NECESSARY LEADERSHIP

Embracing Humility, Upholding Integrity, and Embodying Accountability: An Examination of the Leadership of Rutherford B Hayes

For Nancy,
Thanks so much for the love and support!
Billy

by
BILLY WISNESKI

Published by Author Academy Elite
PO Box 43, Powell, OH 43065
www.AuthorAcademyElite.com

Identifiers:
LCCN: 2023915013
ISBN: 979-8-88583-248-9 (paperback)
ISBN: 979-8-88583-249-6 (hardback)
ISBN: 979-8-88583-250-2 (ebook)

Available in paperback, hardback, e-book

Dedication

For Abby—my necessary life partner and forever love.

FOREWORD

Leadership can take many forms. As a leader, you bare a great responsibility. The results of your leadership may dictate either positive or negative outcomes.

Great leaders are those who, throughout history, have achieved greatness in what their accomplishments and in what they help others to accomplish. Great leaders have many similar characteristics. This book highlights three very important characteristics of solution driven leaders: integrity, humility, and the willingness to be held accountable and in turn, hold others accountable for their actions. Billy Wisneski is a colleague and a friend. In both his personal and professional life, Billy exhibits the characteristics he outlines in *Necessary Leadership*, making him an expert on these topics.

Integrity is often defined as "what you do when no one is watching". However, I believe it is in the watching and analyzing of one's character, that an individual decides if someone is worthy to lead and moreover, followed. Within a person's moral makeup is a small voice or feeling that makes it difficult to follow someone whose morals do not align with yours. If a leader has integrity, you subscribe to the mentality that the leader consistently adheres to a moral code of which you approve.

In today's fast-paced, technology-dependent world, change is rapid. With rapid change, a leader cannot be an expert in every area that impacts their line of work. Humility in leadership is beneficial since humble leaders are not too proud to listen to the opinions or guidance of others. Humble leaders know their strengths, but also know when and where to compliment those strengths, yielding their power for the greater good.

A leader that takes responsibility for positive outcomes as well as mistakes made along the way is crucial for an organization to grow and thrive. Accountability allows for measurement against stated objectives and accountability paired with humility allows for a realistic measurement against those objectives. With humility, leaders are open to changes and improvements, allowing for excellence in achieving stated objectives.

With a lens into the leadership style of Rutherford B Hayes, *Necessary Leadership*, ties the history of a president (whose service was crucial to the shaping of our country) to modern day takeaways for today's leaders. We can all draw from lessons of the past to provide examples of strong leadership qualities that will impact generations to come.

Beth Caravati
Executive Director

AUTHOR'S NOTE

Don't you love the honeymoon phase of a new job? The rejuvenation to get up in the morning and experience something new, learn new things, meet new people. I was in my third year of a job that I enjoyed, working for a boss that I respected, got along well with, and who allowed me to align my daily work with my strengths and passions. Then, a promotion came my way. Something most people would be excited about—a chance to grow, earn more money, and climb the proverbial ladder. After hesitating, talking to mentors, and creating a new budget in my head with a potential raise, I interviewed and received a job offer and accepted the promotion. However, no honeymoon came. I did not enjoy this new work and immediately felt suffocated because I had lost something I had unknowingly relied on for three years—necessary leadership.

During this time, I had been working on a passion project. I love American History—specifically, the Presidency of the United States. Living in Delaware, Ohio, since 2013, I often saw signs or mentions of Rutherford B Hayes, the

19th President of the United States. Even though I had read books or watched every documentary I could on the presidency, Hayes never really came to mind. When I asked others who'd always lived in Delaware about Hayes, no one knew much about him except that there is a high school named Rutherford B Hayes High School and a gas station where his former home was. So, after reading about him and diving into his diary online and at the Rutherford B. Hayes Presidential Library and Museums, I found that Hayes had interesting leadership qualities. During my work experience and reading about Hayes, the idea of leadership began to develop. My project became more about leadership qualities than only Hayes' life and presidency. I could see integrity, humility, and accountability in the decisions that Hayes made and that his leadership style was necessary for his moment in time.

So, that is what this book is about. I hope that leaders of today will understand these qualities and apply them to how they lead. I chose specific stories from Hayes' life and presidency that exemplified those qualities. There is nothing groundbreaking, nor did I provide new, uncovered information about Rutherford B Hayes in the coming pages. This is also not a complete account of Hayes as a person or Hayes the president. My hope is that after reading these pages, the reader is inspired to learn more about this president and his consequential moment in our American Story.

PART I

CHAPTER 1

Leadership requires a level of humility often identified in the gunfire of conflict. A leader who does not embrace a necessary level of humility will fail. So, an arrogant leader (sometimes common in newer leaders) inflicts their personal views onto others, leaving no room for negotiation or conversation, seeks their success and ladders to only their future endeavors, and grandstand about their expertise in the subject matter. An arrogant leader rarely seeks the counsel of others.

In an article published by *Advances in Economics and Business Management*, Rahul Eragula discusses the importance of humility in leadership. Eragula's main objective is comparing, not contrasting, humbleness and arrogance in any organization. Humility can be misinterpreted as low self-esteem and weakness in an aggressive business environment. However, a management expert, Ken Blanchard, "People with humility do not think less of themselves; they just think of themselves less." This is the key difference between arrogance and humility. Eragula states that true success happens when authority meets humility. An arrogant leader pushes responsibilities onto subordinates without delegating authority—they keep that for themselves. According to Eragula, in business terms, an arrogant leader micro-manages, and a culture of micro-managing limits innovation and new ideas, resulting in low productivity.[1] Delegating authority results in higher levels of productivity, happiness among workers, and elevates new leaders. When leaders humble themselves, true authority can thrive.

• • •

In the winter of 1854, members of the Whig Party gathered in Ripon, Wisconsin. The Whig Party, organized in 1834, opposed President Andrew Jackson and won the White House twice. William Henry Harrison and Zachary Taylor were both elected Presidents of the United States as Whigs. John Tyler and Millard Fillmore, both Vice Presidents of the United States at the time of their ascension to the White House, were also Whigs. However, the Kansas-Nebraska Bill of 1854 brought on the demise of the Whig Party in the United States.[2] The bill allowed US territories to decide if slavery would be by popular sovereignty. At the meeting in Ripon, members of the old Whig party founded the Republican Party. In 1856, the first Republican nominee for President of the United States, John C. Fremont of California, lost the election to Democrat James Buchanan of Pennsylvania.[3] A young Civil Rights lawyer from Ohio, Rutherford B. Hayes, closely monitored this election.[4]

Rutherford B. Hayes spent his formative college years at Kenyon College in Gambier, Ohio. Hayes often wrote letters to his uncle, mother, and sister. In June 1841, Hayes decided to start a diary while at Kenyon. The purpose of this diary was to "record my thoughts, desires and resolves" and, in doing so, "promote stability of character." Stability of character was a quality that Hayes was "by no means willing to acknowledge myself deficient." Hayes began this diary to get his thoughts on paper and form conversations he felt unprepared for. In the first diary entries, Hayes spoke of character and self-esteem and stated: "There is perhaps no feature of character of more importance in life than decision." In those days, he affirmed his commitment to becoming decisive.[5]

Decisiveness is a cornerstone for humility. Humility is not a quality one can learn in a classroom or a leadership seminar. Rather, humility rests inside and is cultivated, shaped, and nurtured. The exemplification of humility by true leaders trickles down to those paying attention. These potential leaders decide to allow humility to run their decision-making, and when confronted with conflict, humility triggers conviction to make the right decisions.

In his junior year at Kenyon College, Hayes pursued a law degree. He then decided to stay another year after graduating until he became "a master of logic and rhetoric and to obtain a good knowledge of history." This, Hayes believed, would allow him to be a "tolerable debater." During this period, Hayes hinted_at his ambition to become a public servant. His ambition, although a little ambition is required, did not shadow his humility and his decision to have stability of character. "It is another intention of mine" after graduating law school and practicing law, "to preserve a reputation for honesty and benevolence" and that should he become a public servant, he would "never do anything inconsistent with the character of a true friend and good citizen."[6]

After leaving law school, Hayes established himself in Fremont, Ohio, where his uncle and cousins had already started their business. In the spring of 1845, Hayes spent this time studying and learning from other lawyers. As is common practice in the modern business world, in 1845, new lawyers started at the bottom. They became professionals at what

Hayes wrote, "pettifogging," or having a large workload of petty details. Hayes found himself with better prospects for business than most young lawyers. "I have little competition," Hayes wrote, "taking industry and honesty as among my qualifications" for most lawyers of the area, in Hayes' opinion, "who are responsible or honest are not industrious and vice versa."[7]

Hayes moved to Cincinnati, Ohio, at the beginning of 1850, where his professional and social life started to flourish. Hayes married Lucy Webb in 1852, whose family were sound abolitionists. While on his honeymoon in January 1853, he had a great professional "triumph." Hayes successfully argued his first case in the Ohio Supreme Court. In the case, "State of Ohio v. James Summons," Summons was accused of poisoning his family.[8] This appointment was on the heels of Hayes defending Nancy Farrer, also accused of poisoning two families.

As his professional career flourished in Cincinnati, Hayes began to defend the freedom of blacks. However, with Cincinnati bordering Kentucky, a southern sympathizing state, he did so without seeking publicity. This action may have seemed contrary to his cause. Without seeking publicity, it could be argued that this humble action indicated that the cause mattered more. "My services were always freely given to the slave and his friends in all cases arguing under the Fugitive Slave Law," wrote Hayes.[9] In 1853, Hayes began defending runaway slaves fleeing from Kentucky to Ohio through the Ohio River that divides the two states. The most notable case was Rosetta Armstead, a young girl detained by an antislavery_activist as Armstead was being transferred by her Kentucky owner to Virginia. The antislavery activist from Ohio freed Armstead on a writ of habeas corpus. Armstead's owner appeared in the state and asked the young girl if she wanted to go with him or have freedom. The young girl chose freedom. The owner then had her arrested by a federal marshal.[10]

This case generated a range of legal questions. 1) Does going to a free state automatically make a slave free? 2) Can a state court support the legality of the imprisonment of anyone by a federal marshal? Senator Salmon P. Chase and Judge Timothy Walker defended Armstead, along with Hayes. Although the Hamilton County Court of Common Pleas upheld the writ of habeas corpus, thus freeing Armstead, she was subsequently arrested because the U.S. Commissioner did not want to see federal authority challenged. Hayes defended Armstead by arguing that she was not a runaway since her owner brought her to Ohio. The Commissioner freed Armstead.[11]

In October 1856, as the presidential election campaign neared its end, it was clear that the Republican candidate, John C. Fremont, would to be defeated by Democrat James Buchannan. Hayes wrote, "the good cause has made great progress."[12] Hayes believed that if Fremont had been elected to the presidency, the government would have been placed in the right position to lead the way for antislavery sentiment. Assured, Hayes wrote, "Antislavery sentiment has been created and the people have been educated to a large extent."[11]

Hayes remained determined to rid the country of what he called "the evil." Humility took hold of Hayes, and he vowed to keep working as "further work is to be done." Hayes remembered his sense of duty, not to be in politics for his own glory and success, "but to do what I can consistently with other duties to aid in forming a public opinion on this subject" which will "finally eradicate the evil."[13]

In a journal entry from June 2, 1867, Hayes wrote a letter to "My Darling."[14]

Fremont, June 2, 1867
My Darling,

I reached the depot here about six P.M. yesterday, the boys with Rock met me and had me up to the house in a 'iffy ,' as Mother used to say. Both the boys laughing and talking – as tanned as Indians and jolly as porpoises. Birch chops and hauls dirt for the road and Web rows boat and fishes on the river. School of course but secondary. Their talk was of chickens.

The flower garden has more plants in it and will someday amount to something. Your verbenas (is that right?) will go into a star-shaped bed tomorrow. The rains have brought up the grass everywhere. It is a beautiful place. Birch calls me 'Dad' with great complacency and lays his hand on my shoulder familiarly. Have had a pleasant day with the boys. Very happy little (or big) fellows they are, and happy it is to be with them - Good night. Love to all

Sincerely, your
R.

Humility can be measured by how a superior treats their subordinates. Rutherford B Hayes had eight children with his wife, Lucy Webb Hayes. His children mattered to him. He took them on trips to Washington as a Congressman and while in the White House, made sure to continue their education. Hayes was about to become the Republican nominee for Governor of Ohio in June of 1867. Even during this time, he spent time with his children, all while preparing for a campaign.

CHAPTER 2

Integrity has many definitions. Businesses often use the word in their core values, hopefully representing that the consumer can trust them. Corporations attempt to build their reputation on integrity, and politicians claim their integrity is greater than their opponents. Regarding it, integrity is how an individual or corporation intentionally stands with its morals and values truth. Integrity involves knowing what is right—doing the right thing—knowing it will be difficult.

In *Intentional Integrity: How Smart Companies Lead an Ethical Revolution,* Robert Chestnut, Chief Ethics Officer of Airbnb, provides a road map for leaders to foster a culture of integrity within their company.[15] Chestnut provides the "6 Cs." The first is "C is for Chief." Any company establishing a culture of integrity must start at the top—the boss, the leader, the Chief. This C is first because, without it, nothing else matters. Rules and laws can be written, but if the Chief does not follow these rules, as Chestnut puts it, "you're done." Integrity matters in business and life so people can trust. People trust a person with integrity because they are honest and follow through. They show up during hard times because they said they would.

• • •

"The Southern States are uneasy at the prospect of Lincoln's election today. The ultra south threatens disunion, and it now looks as if South Carolina and possibly? two or three others would go out of the Union?" Hayes wrote on election day, November 6, 1860.[16] On December 20, 1860, South Carolina did just that, becoming the first of ten states to secede from the Union. The Civil War officially began on April 12, 1861, with the attack on Fort Sumter off the coast of South Carolina.

Before the attack of Fort Sumter, Hayes was dispassionate about the southern states seceding. Hayes wrote in his diary on January 4, 1861. "Disunion and civil war are at hand; and yet I fear disunion and war less than compromise. We can recover from them. The free states alone, if we must go on alone, will make a glorious nation."[17] However, after the attack on April 12, the 38-year-old, with three children and another child on the way, was appointed by the governor of Ohio as a major in the 23rd Ohio Volunteers on June 7, 1861. Hayes wrote, "I would prefer to go into it if I knew I was to die or be killed in the course of it, then to live through and after it without taking any part in it."[18] Hayes believed in the cause of the Civil War, believing that the Union States were on the right side of history. The truest example of integrity is fighting for your beliefs. Hayes believed in the Civil War and picked up the armor to fight in it.

Hayes quickly earned the respect of his fellow soldiers by calming soldiers who refused to accept old muskets and his actions in the field. The most notable account was during the battle of South Mountain on September 14, 1862.

Confederate armies owned the summit of the mountain where the old National Road crossed it. Lieutenant-Colonel Hayes was ordered to open the engagement with the Confederates by advancing up the mountain path. When Hayes saw the Confederate army, the company advanced forcefully with a yell, and although they took on enemy fire, drove the Confederates out of the woods into an opening. After Hayes gave three commands to charge, he felt a blow to his left arm. He had been hit by a musket ball which badly fractured his entire bone. Fearing a ruptured artery, Hayes had a soldier bandage up his arm, then collapsed from exhaustion. After regaining consciousness, Hayes had found that his men had sheltered in the woods around him, and he quickly sprang to action, calling them back to battle. They followed him. Hayes continued to lead his men in the fight until he collapsed again, where he continued giving orders from the ground. Major Comly, the second-in-command, then took charge and ordered Lieutenant-Colonel Hayes carried from the field. Hayes recalls, while lying on the battlefield, wounded by a Confederate bullet, "While I was down I had a considerable talk with a wounded Confederate lying near me. I gave him messages for my wife and friends in case I should not get up. We were right jolly and friendly. It was by no means an unpleasant experience."[19] During an intense display of integrity, leading his men in a battle he believed in, fought in, and was injured in against an enemy, Hayes showed humility with that same enemy.

Hayes was promoted to Colonel and, throughout 1863 and 1864, regularly commanded a brigade fighting alongside his men. Later, he became a major general but reminded his diary that he never fought as a general, stating, "Of course I know that my place was a very humble one—I also am glad to know that I was one of the good colonels."[20] A title Hayes was not expecting while fighting in the Civil War was Congressman. During the final battles of the war August

6, 1864, Hayes was nominated as the Republican candidate for the Second District of Ohio to the United States House of Representatives. The nomination was not by Haye's own doing but solely contrived by his friends back home. After learning of the nomination in a letter, Hayes wrote back, "an officer fit for duty who at this crisis would abandon his post to electioneer for a seat in Congress ought to be scalped."[21] Hayes believed he had a duty to finish what he started. He had a duty to his men, his cause, and his country to stay in the army. After a victorious battle at Cedar Creek in the Shenandoah Valley in October 1865, Hayes learned he was victorious in another fashion—he was elected to the 39th United States House of Representatives as the Congressman from the Second District of Ohio.

• • •

"It now looks as if I would not consent to run for governor,"[22] Hayes wrote to his uncle in May 1867 when serving as a congressman for the second district of Ohio. During his term as a congressman, many people inquired about his interest to run for Governor of Ohio. Hayes believed his constituents elected him to serve them in Congress and that he should not seek another position while already serving in an elected office. Those who wanted Hayes to run for Governor believed his leadership was required to take Ohio to the next level and attempted to flatter his ego as much as possible.

Hayes demonstrated further leadership characteristics that same year. Also, in 1867, Ohio's Governor, Jacob Dolson Cox, decided not to run for re-election. Hayes had not shown any need for "Congressional reputation or influence."[23] Hayes, faithful to his constituents of the second district, was not interested in running for Governor. Before Cox's decision not to run for re-election (after serving two terms as governor), Hayes relied on the advice and desires of his constituents. Hayes made this clear in a letter to Ohio's Secretary of State, William Henry Smith, responding to Smith's request that Hayes run for Governor. On January 26, 1867, Hayes wrote: "Since General Cox's declination one or two persons, in a merely casual way, have spoken to me on the subject. Your letter contains the first and only serious suggestion of the sort I have received from Ohio."[24] His constituents wanted him to stay in Congress and represent them. This show of passion for doing what his constituents wanted and determination to fulfill what he was elected to do shows the integrity required for leadership. Although there may have been a slight consideration by Hayes to run for a higher office, he put his constituents first. "Having been elected by the Union people of the Second District to an office which they knew I wanted," Hayes continues to Smith, "It would not be right to resign it without their approval."[25]

Integrity also means recognizing the existence of other perspectives and opinions worth exploring. Hayes made it clear that he "...would not go into a contest with another Union man of Hamilton County for the support of the delegation of that county."[26] Unlike many politicians today, Hayes did not see the point in running for and then leaving an office without the desire and approval of "the party and its public men." Hayes wanted the nominee to be backed by everyone and did not have the desire to grandstand. He believed he was the right choice for the job if everyone else also believed he was the right choice for the job.

By February of 1867, Hayes was adamant that his name not be thrown into the convention. Although friends and party leaders pushed his nomination, constituents did not agree. That was enough for Hayes to decide not to run. However, on learning of Hayes' refusal to run, William Henry Smith immediately wrote to Hayes stomping out any of Hayes' reservations. He had full support of the party and would run seemingly unopposed. The nomination was his if he wanted it. "It was the opinion of all the best men that you were the only one who could carry us safely and triumphantly through the campaign,"[27] said Smith. Along with the support and his "chief personal objection" to running for Governor—the Legislature standing up to the suffrage issue, Hayes consented to the nomination.

CHAPTER 3

Accountability is a scary word. It often carries a connotation with punishment. Often, people shy away from accountability to avoid potential failure. Failure and accountability need not go hand in hand. What if accountability was used as a tool for self-improvement rather than self-sabotage?

Jonathan Raymond wrote about two hidden beliefs people mistakenly embrace regarding accountability. The first is the interrelation between accountability and punishment. The second is that accountability is only seen as a one-time event rather than a long-term habit. Combating those hidden beliefs is difficult since they often manifest themselves when someone seeks accountability. On the other hand, someone might encounter one experience where having an accountability partner exceeded expectations, and they grew from the experience. Raymond's experience shows that leaders hold accountability in high regard. They want to keep their employees accountable. However, this faulty accountability concept often exists in the two hidden beliefs, thereby depriving employees from growth potential.[28]

Accountability does not necessarily have to have those negative connotations. Seeking accountability does not necessarily mean a person expects punishment if they do not complete assigned tasks. Accountability can and should provide good fruits in life. The first step is wanting accountability and knowing how you will best respond, whether sticking to a workout or job performance. When we seek out those who hold us accountable without incorporating the two hidden beliefs of accountability, we progress in following through with tasks and goals and can see success at the end of the day.

• • •

"Came here as a member of the House of Representatives for Second District of Ohio this morning,"[29] Rutherford B Hayes wrote on November 30, 1865 in Washington, D.C. The following day, December 1, 1865, a caucus of Ohio Union delegation agreed to "oppose the admission of any delegates from the Rebel States for the present"[30] along with a proposal from General Schenck "an amendment on the first opportunity by which representation would be based on suffrage," wrote Hayes. Hayes continued upon the suggestion of General Schenck. "I offered the resolution with educational test or condition added." Immediately Hayes began his work in Congress focusing on his primary election objective—to protect the Union he fought for and to bring Civil Rights to the forefront of his time in office.[31]

When Hayes joined Congress in December 1865, he faced an interesting set of circumstances. In April 1865, President Abraham Lincoln, a Republican, was assassinated, making Lincoln's Vice-President, Andrew Johnson, President. Andrew Johnson was a Democrat who immediately sought to oppose the new Republican Congress agenda. Hayes worked during his terms in Congress to maintain the Union he fought for, keeping the president's actions accountable in attempts to give congressional rebels their way on preventing passage of suffrage legislation or enacting laws circumventing rights granted to blacks in the South.

Hayes opposed running for Governor of Ohio. However, again engineered by his friends, Rutherford B Hayes was nominated as the Republican candidate for Governor. Hayes believed that he should stay in Congress. After all, the constituencies of the Second District in Cincinnati voted for him to do so. Hayes felt he should be accountable to them. However, after William Henry Smith convinced him that "all of the best men"[32] thought Hayes was the right person for the moment. When the Ohio Legislature proposed an amendment to the Constitution, extending the right to vote to blacks, Hayes' "chief person objection" was removed.

Hayes' campaign had two major focuses: advocating for the black suffrage amendment and defending the "radical Republican" agenda. The Democratic reconstruction agenda pushed confederate, independent states. Hayes advocated for a united Union. In a campaign speech on August 5, 1867, in Lebanon, Ohio, Hayes began by quoting Lincoln's Gettysburg Address. "Four score and seven years ago our fathers brought forth on this continent a new Nation, conceived in liberty and dedicated to the proposition that all men are created equal."[33] Hayes proposed this was Lincoln's interpretation of the Declaration of Independence's meaning—the birth of a nation dedicated to equal rights. The importance of those words was not hidden to someone of intelligence. "Their language is simple, their meaning plain, and their truth undoubtful."[34] Hayes called out the rebels' attempt to destroy the founding fathers' "fundamental truth of the Declaration of Independence by limiting the application of the phrase 'all men' to *the* men of a single race."[35] Others did not always meet these views of suffrage with the same affirmation delivered by Hayes during his campaign. In fact, Hayes' views were unpopular in parts of the state, but always consistent in his message and beliefs, Hayes was able to convince enough voters to elect him the governor of Ohio.

In his inaugural address on January 13, 1868, Hayes addressed his vision for Ohio and his purpose as Governor. He addressed four major issues in the shortest inaugural address ever made by a governor of Ohio at the time: taxation based on the size of property owned, too much legislation, civil rights equality, and the Fourteenth Amendment to the National Constitution. Hayes addressed civil rights and the ratification of the Fourteenth Amendment during most of his address, making it clear he was elected Governor of all Ohioans and would assist in the suffrage of black people nationally. The voters would keep him accountable in these tasks.

Although the legislature and his former congressional seat in the Second District had gone to the Democrats, Hayes was generally satisfied with his position as Governor. Hayes wrote to his uncle. "I am enjoying the new office. It strikes me at a guess as the pleasantest I have ever had. Not too much hard work, plenty of time to read, good society, etc."[36] The Democrats did not make Hayes' legislative life easy, however. On January 15, 1868, the new General Assembly quickly reversed the previous General Assembly's vote on the Fourteenth Amendment and reminded Ohio's ratification of the amendment. Since the governor of Ohio did not have veto power, Hayes had to watch the vote pass. However, the Fourteenth Amendment became part of the National Constitution, with the federal government ignoring the General Assembly's vote.

Since the legislature was unwilling to work with Hayes on the main points of his inaugural address, he carried on with what he could do as Governor, including completing an asylum for those with disabilities and establishing a girls' reform school. Hayes also set out to acquire many portraits of former governors to display in the state house. It was in National politics that Hayes found his new office most useful. He conferred with Indiana Republicans on currency issues and weighed in the impending impeachment trial of President Andrew Johnson. Johnson had been charged with violating the Tenure of Office Act. Hayes received a telegraph from J.C. Lee, asking the governor: "What do Ohio Republicans desire as to impeachment? Answer fully." The Governor's full response back was "Conviction."[37] The House of Representatives impeached the president in February 1868.

After the impeachment, in which the Senate acquitted Johnson by one vote, Hayes threw himself into the 1868 Presidential election. The Republicans nominated General Ulysses S. Grant and Schuyler Colfax of Indiana for Vice President, and Hayes was actively involved in the campaign to take Ohio by storm. The work paid off; Grant won the 1868 Presidential Election November 3, 1868. Excited about the new possibilities that a Republican President could bring to the country, Hayes was eager to meet with him. In a letter Hayes wrote to his uncle on December 19, 1868, he describes his time spent with Grant. "Got home safe this morning," Hayes wrote. "Had a good time. The most satisfactory part of the trip was serval hours' quiet time with General Grant. It was most delightful talk. After he warms up he is...quite as cheerful, chatty, and good-natured, and so sensible, clear-headed, and well-informed. I feel just as much at was with him as I do with intimate friends...This sounds strange, but I mention it because it will give you an idea how completely and wonderfully he remains unspoiled by his elevation."[38] Hayes' time with the newly elected president allowed him to assess his ability to hold the president accountable on his campaign issues. Hayes had an agenda to expand the black suffrage movement nationally and to maintain the Union that he fought for. Hayes could see success in this new president.

On December 7, 1868, the 40th Congress of the United States introduced a resolution proposing an amendment to the Constitution of the United States. The resolution read, "Section 1. The right of citizens of the United States to vote shall not be denied or abridged by the United States or by and State on account of race, color, or previous condition of servitude—Section 2. The Congress shall have the power to enforce this article by appropriate legislation."[39] This resolution was the Fifteenth Amendment to the Constitution, granting black males the right to vote in the United States. As Hayes was gearing up to run for reelection as Governor of Ohio, the Fifteenth Amendment was part of his campaign. The General Assembly in Ohio had denied the amendment on May 4, 1869. However, Hayes believed a Republican majority would be elected for the next assembly, providing enough votes to ratify the amendment. The election on October 12, 1869, appeared to be close to a tie between Hayes and the Democrat George Hunt Pendleton for most of the day and into the next. Hayes was relaxed and at peace with whatever the outcome would be. "I am laughing and serene as usual" Hayes wrote to his uncle on October 13, the day after election day, "but there are anxious faces over the figures," he continued.[40] With a margin of 7,501, Hayes was reelected as Governor of Ohio. The Republicans also gained control of the legislature by a narrow margin.

As he did for his first inaugural address, Hayes wrote out his vision and objectives for the coming term—first, the Fifteenth Amendment. The previous assembly had rejected it, but Hayes was counting on the next assembly to ratify it. Next, he focused on reforming laws previous legislatures enacted in soldiers' orphans' homes and prison disciplines. Hayes also focused on the geological survey, places of refuge for "inebriates" and the "incurable insane." Finally, he wanted to look at the development and placement of the Agricultural and Mechanical College provided by Justin Smith and Morrill's Land Grant. Hayes built his vision on the foundation of the maxim "that government is best which governs least." Although laying out his vision for Ohio with programs formed by the government, Hayes believed that the best results are when "every department of government is kept within its own sphere and every officer performs faithfully his own duty without magnifying his office." When that happens "harmony, efficiency, and economy will prevail."[40]

Hayes' second term as Governor was much more successful than his first. As Republican legislators, they were more willing to work with Hayes and move forward with his agenda. To keep true to the maxim and remain accountable to those that put him in office to make the difference he promised, Hayes' priority was to secure the ratification of the fifteenth amendment. By the slimmest of margins, Ohio ratified the amendment. On March 30, 1870, the fifteenth amendment was added to the Constitution of the United States when three-fourths of the states had ratified it. During his second term, the legislature also established the Agricultural and Mechanical College, later called The Ohio State University. Maintaining a desirable amount of bipartisanship and accountability during the board formation for the college, Hayes tapped George Hunt Pendleton, his former opponent for Governor. Hayes was unsuccessful in getting Pendleton to serve on the board.

The term of Governorship of Ohio in Hayes' time was two years, but not limited to two terms. However, Hayes was done with politics. He had jested in the early days of his second term after the ratification of the fifteenth amendment (a major personal triumph), "I too mean to be out of politics. The ratification of the Fifteenth Amendment gives me the boon of equality before the law, terminates my enlistment, and discharges me cured."[41] With the triumph of the fifteen amendment, the establishment of the geological survey, the Agricultural and Mechanical College, the soldiers and sailors' orphans home, Hayes felt he had done his job as Governor and looked forward to retirement. However, retirement would not be that simple. Hayes was on everyone's mind as the next Senator of Ohio and probably the next president of the United States. Another term as Governor was still on the table for some of the Republican party, but Hayes threw his support into his next, hand-picked successor, John Sherman.

Accountability is both messy and necessary. In his first few elected positions, Hayes first held himself accountable. He ran campaigns based on what he felt was best for his congressional district and State. When elected to those positions, he fought for what he campaigned for and put people around him that did not necessarily have the same point of view. Hayes was able to run for reelection based on a record that proved he would do as promised and if the people did not want to elect him, they did not have to vote for him.

PART II

INTRODUCTION

Presidential elections in modern US politics consist of primaries and caucuses held in each state. Sometimes in an election campaign year there is a caucus or primary in only one state The first and most famous is the Iowa caucus. This is possibly the make-or-break moment for any political campaign. The winning candidate gains a huge boost in campaign momentum. However, winning the Iowa caucus does not guarantee winning the party's respective nomination nor does it mean the winner has the greatest chance to become president. Since 1976, only three presidents that won the Iowa caucus became president of the United States: Jimmy Carter in 1976, George W. Bush in 2000 and Barack Obama in 2008.[42]

Then there are Super Tuesdays. These are Tuesdays in the primary and caucus calendar that will hold multiple state primaries and caucus elections. In the case of the 2020 presidential election, where there was only a primary contest for the Democratic nominee, Tuesday, March 3, 2020, was Super Tuesday. That Tuesday alone totaled the possibility of 1,357 delegates. In 2020, a candidate needed 1,991 unpledged delegates to win the Democratic nomination. Primaries or caucuses on March 3 were Alabama, Arkansas, California, Colorado, Maine, Massachusetts, Minnesota, North Carolina, Oklahoma, Tennessee, Texas, Utah, Virginia, Vermont, and American Samoa.[43]

A party's presidential convention today is mostly a celebration of their nominee. The nominee is chosen long before the convention begins. The convention gives the candidate the opportunity to accept the nomination and stand on the platform developed during the week by the party delegates.

In 1876, Democrat and Republican candidates did not have primaries and caucuses. They did not have Super Tuesdays. Their first chance to promote themselves was at the convention where delegates chosen by party bosses nominated their favored candidates. A roll call was then taken, and the delegates from each state voted for their candidate. The winner needed to win the majority (51%) of delegates to become the nominee. This process took as many ballots as necessary. In June 1876, in Cincinnati, Ohio, the Republican delegates were gathering for their convention, getting ready seemingly to nominate James G. Blaine.

President Ulysses S. Grant was running out of time.

CHAPTER 1

Having served for eight years as President of the United States, he considered running for an unprecedented third term. In 1875, the twenty-second Amendment to the United States Constitution did not exist. That Amendment would not be ratified into the Constitution until 1951, after President Franklin Delano Roosevelt made history when elected to his fourth term as President. However, he only served three full terms due to his April 12, 1945 death. Until Roosevelt, the men elected to be President of the United States followed the standard set by George Washington; they would, if reelected, serve two terms and step aside, allowing for the peaceful transfer of power.

Grant was popular in factions of the Republican party. When rumors of scandals started swirling as the time to decide to run for reelection drew nearer, some of that support dwindled. Although the rumors did not provide evidence of Grant's guilt, nevertheless, scandal was a stain on any candidacy. On the counsel of his supporters and a supportive wife, Grant chose not to seek a consecutive third term. "I do not want to be here another four years," Grant would say about the prospect of a third term. "I do not think I could stand it."[44] He made his decision and would not run, *yet*.

Grant's decision not to run served as the catalyst for a dramatic campaign cycle and a contentious general election that resulted in a constitutional crisis, unlike anything before or since. The fractured Republican party selected the governor from Ohio, Rutherford B Hayes as its nominee. The Democratic party, seeing an opportunity to pounce on the scandals from the Grant administration, nominated the governor of New York, Samuel Tilden. The Republican party had controlled the White House since Abraham Lincoln's inauguration in 1861. The American public tired of reconstruction, and the Democrats thought they had a chance to seize power.

With twenty hotly contested electoral college votes, Rutherford B Hayes took the highest office in the land despite losing the popular vote. Faced with reconstruction, a divided country, and the public perception that he stole the election, strife marked the beginning of his presidency. His past, however, had primed him to lead. He had served as the governor of Ohio, a U.S. Congressman, and a civil rights lawyer. Most importantly, Hayes had a heart for the country for which he had fought as a Union soldier during the Civil War. Rutherford B Hayes was ready for the next step in his career as the nineteenth President of the United States of America.

Spring 1875 in Spiegel Grove, Ohio.

CHAPTER 2

Rutherford B Hayes observed the land given to him by his Uncle Sardis, who died on January 21, 1874. The maples began to show their reddish-brown leaves. The oak trees were still bare. The elms "show the coming events a little. "We saw the first green trees on the place yesterday, the buckeyes in [the] garden. The leaves on the apple trees are beginning to show,"[45] Hayes wrote in his diary. Hayes spent most of his energy in retirement on Spiegel Grove, planting fruit, nut trees, evergreens, berries, and a vegetable garden. It has been almost three years since Hayes retired from politics, leaving the governor's office on January 8, 1872. The excitement of retiring to a quieter life with Lucy is scribed by his own hand as "we go out today 'joyfully, joyfully' as little Fan sings."[46] However, now, his party and his state are calling him back. "The first cherries in bloom yesterday. No tree in sight of the house shows a solid green. The little apple trees and early harvest show the most green,"[47] he discerned.

"I was nominated for governor yesterday at Columbus,"[48] Hayes penned in his diary on June 3, 1875. Until his actual nomination, he declined interest in running when asked. Hayes knew that Judge Alphonso Taft of Cincinnati was gunning for the nomination. With respect and confidence in Taft, Hayes would not purposely seek to wrestle the nomination from him. Reluctancy to give up retirement was not Hayes' only motivation to not to seek the governor's office for a third time. The talk was that Hayes would be the Republican nominee for President of the United States in 1876 if he was willing to run. "How wild! What a queer lot we are becoming. No body is out of the reach of that mania."[49] Hayes responded to the idea of the presidency. Of course, Hayes would win his election to be Governor of Ohio by 5,544 votes, and at least ten Ohio newspapers published articles to support his presidency. Although Hayes found the idea silly and the thought of disrupting his quiet life with Lucy unappealing, he could not stop the political forces from pulling him into office again.

As another gubernatorial term began, so did the chatter of an eventual nomination for the Republican candidate for President of the United States. Hayes' view on the candidacy remained consistent with his previous candidacies—he would not seek it outright. If there is a better person to be the candidate, (and he believed there was), they should be the candidate. In a letter to his good friend Guy Bryan, Hayes wrote, "My rule as Governor was to obey the Eleventh commandment to the letter. I never alluded even to general politics except when my State was to act on an amendment to the National Constitution." Now, the eleventh commandment would be to support Blaine for the candidacy that he would do. Ending his letter to Bryan, Hayes confessed, "a sty on one of my eyelids prevents me from writing with comfort."[51] Although painful to Hayes at that moment, the sty would foreshadow the upcoming convention and election.

Cincinnati was bustling with excitement.[52]

CHAPTER 3

Delegates for the National Republican Convention were entering the town with gusto as they prepared to market their candidate to undecided delegates. The prominent candidates, Secretary of the Treasury Benjamin H Bristow, Speaker of the House James G. Blaine, and Senator of Indiana Oliver P. Morton, all had headquarters in the city to campaign for their candidates. Hotel fronts were illuminated with campaign slogans. The campaign for Rutherford B. Hayes of Ohio was not as brazen. They, too, had their share of campaign paraphernalia but were not as audacious. As the convention week began, fireworks were displayed, strangers became friends, and, most importantly, the campaign workers were pounding the pavement. Workers representing candidates were swirling the crowds making promises, taking bribes, trying to win over delegates to their candidates' corner; the hard, necessary work to win the nomination.

It was clear to many that James Blaine was the man to beat. His supporters were confident of 300 votes on the first ballot, making it difficult for any other candidate to chip away at that support. Blaine's campaign workers seemed to have an easy job ahead of them for persuading undecided delegates would be simple—Blaine was the clear nominee, jump on this campaign now and this convention will be over. The workers spoke of Blaine's intelligence, his brilliance, and ability in the House to unnerve the rebels. The workers campaigned on a foundation that Blaine would make the Rebels to take back seats should he become President. The workers were good at their job that they never mentioned the facts that could potentially hurt a candidate in the general election. Blaine was Speaker of the House from 1869-1875 when the railroad schemes, which he had interests in, pushed through the chamber. Nor was there mention of the speculating in stocks that required Congressional legislation that, of course, Blaine held votes on. Blaine had also had a stroke. However, in 1876, negatively speaking of someone's health was deemed inappropriate.

The work of the convention had begun. After the committees had all met, the platform had been created, and the nomination process began. As a roll of the states was called, the states were allowed to call a candidate for nomination. The rules allowed for a ten-minute speech and required a second. In all, ten nominated candidates made the ballot for the Republican nominee for President of the United States: Blaine, Morton, Conkling, Bristow, Hartranft, Hayes, Wheeler, Washburne, Jewell, and Clark.

Delegates came to conventions with a priority: they would vote for their candidate on the first ballot. Then, the real task of the campaign workers would begin. Delegates could switch their vote to another candidate. Oftentimes, candidates would withdraw their name following a ballot due to a lack of votes and a clear path to victory. If the campaign workers succeeded, delegates would fall in line and vote for the worker's candidates. Clearly, Morton, Conkling, Hartrant, and Jewell would not make it to the nomination. Therefore, those delegates would either vote for Bristow or Hayes. Disdain rose for Blaine due to the influence of liberal perpetrators and newspapers running articles against Blaine. Delegates that may appear to be undecided were becoming more and more against Blaine as the nominee. As Conklin dropped, delegates would go for either Bristow or Hayes, not Blaine.

By the fourth ballot, Bristow was gaining ground, but so was Blaine with 126 and 292, respectively. Hayes stood at 68 on the fourth ballot. Blaine lost votes on the fifth ballot, bringing him to 286, the lowest he had ever collected since the first ballot. Seeing a dip in Blaine's support and a zero gain for Bristow, states started taking their delegates away from the top two candidates and giving them to Hayes. By the seventh ballot, Morton, Conkling, and Hartranft withdrew, handing their delegates to Hayes. The delegate count stood thus: Hayes 384, Blaine 351, Bristow 21. The cheering lasted for 20 minutes when Hayes' nomination was unanimous.[53] William A. Wheeler would be nominated for Vice President. Hayes later wrote, "I am ashamed to say: Who is Wheeler?"[54]

In his letter after the convention and to the American people, Hayes accepted the nomination on the foundation of the platform created at the convention without reservation. The platform for the Republican party in 1876 recognized the substantial advances toward establishing equal rights for women. The platform requested that additional rights, privileges, and immunities regarding the demands on women should be considered. In 1876 America, women did not have the right to vote and would not until the ratification of the 19th Amendment. The Amendment passed the Congress on June 4, 1919, and was ratified on August 18, 1920.

Hayes particularly reflected on the fifth resolution adopted by the convention. The fifth resolution supported that, according to constitutional law, the president, and departments heads would make nominations for office with advice and consent from the Senate, and the job of accusation and prosecution of faithless officers rested with the House of Representatives. Hayes argued that this principle laid out here has become null and void. The appointment of officers resulted in Congressional members providing jobs to party faithfuls. Hayes promised to bring back the principles of honesty, capacity, and fidelity as the only qualifications for holding office.

In a stark contrast to previous nominees and to those that followed, Hayes made another promise in his acceptance speech—one term[55]:

> "The declaration of principals by the Cincinnati convention makes no announcement in favor of a simple presidential term. I do not assume to add to that declarations but believing that the restoration of the civil service to the system established by Washington and followed by the early presidents can be best accomplished by an executive who is under no temptation to use the patronage of his office to promote his own re-election, I desire to perform what I regard as a duty, in stating now my inflexible purpose, if elected, not to be a candidate for election to a second term."

Hayes would be only the second president to fulfill the promise of being a one-term president. James Polk, the 11th President of the United States, completed only one term as promised. William Henry Harrison would also make the one-term President pledge. However, he died 31 days into his presidency as the ninth President of the United States, making history as the shortest presidency and never getting the chance to fulfill his one-term pledge. Many men and women running for President make the one-term presidency pledge. Often, those individuals do not make it to the office they seek. When they do, that pledge seems to get lost. The trappings of the presidency become too awesome. Power—too great to give up.

They soon fell into a refreshing sleep, and,
at that moment, it all seemed over.

CHAPTER 4

With the candidates selected for both parties, the election of 1876 was underway. The Democrats nominated Samuel Tilden, the sitting Governor of New York. Tilden was a popular Governor of New York known for his reform policies and anti-corruption stance. Tilden was pivotal in the "Tweed Ring" in 1871, uncovering evidence of corruption.[56] While serving as Governor, Tilden worked to break up the "Canal Ring," created for individuals to illegally make millions of dollars from contracts for repairing and expanding New York State's canal system. With reform and the attitude to break up corruption, Tilden was a formidable candidate.

As campaigns go, the campaign of 1876 was not shy of roorbacks. Hayes was attacked for supposed hostility toward foreigners as voters and office holders. Hayes argued his record and pointed out his voting record for naturalized citizens and having appointed them to office. He had worked to keep schools free of sectarian influence, and Hayes was constantly reassuring the public of his lack of prejudiced against any religion. Not actively campaigning himself,

Hayes' surrogates were not shielded from campaign smears. Hayes had to write to General Carl Schurz to reassure him that Hayes still wanted him to stump. A roorback had been floating that William E Chandler demanded Schurz stop making campaign speeches. "There is surely no foundation for it. But in any event, I desire that you speak," said Hayes. "Governor Morton desires it. The party desires it. The people generally who approve our principles desire it, and no man can say nay to it." Hayes' tax returns came in to focus and were examined. The returns showed that in 1868 and 1869, Hayes "made none at all."[57] The taxable income of the then governor of Ohio was "fifteen hundred or twenty-five hundred dollars." Hayes' explained that more than likely no returns were called for. However, should there be a return and payment required, it would be paid.

In his nomination acceptance letter, Hayes declared his intention to seek only one term as President. Hayes intended this declaration to proclaim that he would not use his time as president to campaign for another term but would pursue fulfillment of his campaign promises without the ambition to run again. At the time, this proclamation was unprecedented and drew some skepticism from the opposition. The proclamation also provided some unintended offense from Hayes' own party, particularly the current Republican president. Ulysses S. Grant found Hayes' intent to serve for one term an opportunity to differentiate himself from Grant, and that Grant's previous choice to run for a second term displayed poor character. Haye's quickly wrote to Grant to reassure the president. "Nothing, I assure you, is further from the fact," said Hayes to Grant. Hayes' intent to run for one term, Hayes explains, is it allows his fellow candidates the opportunity to run for the nomination again in 1880, given that Hayes was the older candidate and was not the prominent candidate outside of his state. "It seemed to be therefore that nominated as I was, it would tend to unite and harmonize their friends if it were certainly known that I would not be in their way four years from now,"[58] Hayes opined. Hayes believed that the one-term promise would strengthen his administration. The letter appeared to calm the tension between Grant and Hayes.

The October 1876 elections would be a temperature gauge for the November 1876 elections and the presidential results. Ohio went to the Republicans by 9,000 votes which Hayes believed would double in November. However, in Indiana, the Democrats won by 5,000. Although optimistic about the chances of a Republican pull-off in Indiana, Hayes believed that the focus needed to turn to New York, Tilden's home state, or garner enough electoral votes from the Carolinas, Florida, Mississippi, and Louisiana. The ramifications of the Civil War were still in effect in the South. Reconstruction saw the implant of federal troops in southern states to protect Republican votes and Republican administrators from those that sought violence as an intimidation tactic to repress the Republican vote—the *black* Republican vote. Murder was the most prominent intimidation tactic used. After the loss in Indiana, the Grant Administration increased the amount of federal troops in the South. There were already 2,800 troops in the eleven former Confederate states.[59]

Hayes remained optimistic but realistic in his evaluation of the election and its results two weeks before the election. "I am surprised, whenever I think of it, to find myself so cool, so almost indifferent about it."[60] The thought of the government going to the Democrats kept him motivated and clear-minded. However, Hayes saw a potential defeat as a blessing. Having long wanted to be retired from politics, that would be his chance to move on and live a quieter life. With unknowing foresight, Hayes laments of another danger in the election—a contested election outcome. Hayes believed that no presidential election should occur without a clear means of legally settling a contested result. He forecasted this possibility: "it may lead to a conflict of arms," and he know that preventing another Civil War was a priority. Even after traveling through Ohio and celebrating Ohio Day at the Centennial with supportive and enthusiastic crowds, Hayes returned home believing a loss was on the horizon. Fraud from the North and violence in the South would skew the election to Tilden, according to Hayes, "But I have made a good fight: sound Letter to stand on"[60] and a steady and level head gave Hayes the optimism he needed to finish out the campaign.

Election Day, November 7, 1876, was cold and dry but perfect for election work. Hayes was confident about the results but mentally reserved the possible Democratic victory. If that victory was at hand, the South would surely suffer the most. If Tilden was elected, Hayes believed, the South would suffer in deterioration of civil service. The South would drift back into chaos.

Business would be fine. Government, in the judgment of Hayes, did not make business prosperity. Election Day would not provide the result Hayes was hoping for. In fact, it provided no result. A party had gathered in the parlor of the Hayes residence as some results had started to trickle in. Although the party atmosphere began to diminish somewhat, Hayes kept his composure and was even cheerful. Lucy, however, busied herself by getting refreshments. Alas, Lucy's anxiety got the best of her, leaving her in bed with a headache. Around midnight, Hayes went to bed and consoled Lucy. They discussed their personal acceptance in losing the election, but they lamented what this might mean for the South.

The next day, Wednesday, November 8, 1876, a contented and cheerful Hayes heard received the election results. Hayes carried California, Oregon, and all of New England except for Connecticut. With the "freed states" also in Hayes' column (Ohio, Pennsylvania, Illinois, Michigan, Wisconsin, Iowa, Minnesota, Nebraska, Kansas, Colorado, and Nevada) and the potential for some Southern states that Hayes believed he had a chance in, a victory was in sight. New York was still undeclared. With the excitement of a potential victory starting to stir within him, Hayes made a statement attempting to tamper the flurry of incoming messages. "It is impossible, at so early a time, to obtain the result, owing to the incomplete telegraph communications through some of the Southern and Western States,"[61] Hayes stated. Probably attempting to tamper his own mounting excitement and attempting to maintain a level of humility, Hayes continued, "if it should not be successful, I shall surely have the pleasure of living for the next year and a half among some of my most ardent and enthusiastic friends."[62]

The news continued to hold the country's attention. Victory claims came from the Republicans that the Hayes campaign had won Louisiana, South Carolina, and Florida. This claim earned the Hayes-Wheeler ticket 185 electoral votes. On the other hand, the *Louisiana Democrat,* , declared in their November 15 issue that "Samuel J. Tilden, of New York, and Thomas A. Hendricks, of Indiana, are elected President and Vice President of the United States!" with Tilden receiving 203 electoral votes. The paper went on to say their readers could be confident the report was most reliable and correct and to even save the paper for future reference.

Neither party's victory projections were accurate. The Democrats saw victory in their grasp with the announcement of Tilden's 4,288,546 popular votes compared with Hayes' 4,034,311 popular votes. However, a US president is elected by winning the most electoral college votes, *not* the popular vote majority. Concerns arose when Florida, South Carolina, and Louisiana—all with Republican governors—delayed reporting the official vote count. Both Democrats and Republicans sent representatives, which became "returning boards", to the three states to review the election. The returning boards discovered improper voting practices and disallowed ballots. The boards determined the following: if "repeaters" were used to stuff the ballot boxes; if illiterate black voters could not determine for whom they were voting, if black voters were intimidated at the polls, thereby keeping the Republican vote lower; and even if ballot boxes were hidden away and more ballots added later in secret. When the investigation began, the unofficial vote was:

Florida – Tilden 24,433; Hayes 24,340,
Louisiana – Tilden 83,723; Hayes 77,174
South Carolina – Tilden 90,896; Hayes 91,870

When the returning boards finished their investigation, the certified vote counts for the three states were:

Florida – Tilden 22,927; Hayes 23,894
Louisiana – Tilden 70,508; Hayes 75,313
South Carolina – Tilden 90,896; Hayes 91,870

These amended voting returns awarded Hayes 185 electoral votes and Tilden 184 electoral vote counts, making Rutherford B Hayes President of the United States.[63]

The presidential election process now continued. With the electoral votes certified by the states, usually the president of the Senate (the sitting vice-president) then certifies the states' electoral votes. But another wrench was thrown into the process in the 1876 election. Vice president Henry Wilson had died in 1875. Senator Thomas Ferry, a Republican from Michigan, replaced Wilson as Senate president. Ferry decided that he alone should not preside over the certification, citing the Constitution's requirement that the vice president be the Senate president. To resolve the dispute, the House and Senate created the Electoral Commission in December 1876. The group was comprised of five senators, five representatives of the House, and five

Supreme Court justices. There were eight Republicans and seven Democrats. Electoral Commission hearings began on February 1, 1877, and during the next four weeks, the group discussed each disputed state election. In the end, Hayes received the electoral vote for each state.[64]

It was not finished, but work needed to start.

CHAPTER 5

The electoral vote count had yet to finish when Hayes and his wife began their journey to Washington, D.C., on Thursday, March 1, 1877. The presumptive First Couple left Columbus, Ohio, around noon after being escorted by the college cadets to the train station. A short speech by the presumptive President on a "special car" attached to a regular passenger train would take them from Ohio to Washington, D.C. The journey was filled with throngs of enthusiastic crowds in Newark, Dennison, and Steubenville. In the middle of the night, on March 2, 1877, the couple had been awakened by the news that the electoral college count had been completed. Rutherford B Hayes was now the president-elect of the United States of America. Just three days before President Ulysses S Grant's term ended, Hayes would be inaugurated.

The completion of the election was not the end of animosity towards Hayes. Hayes entered his presidency after a contested election, an election involving violence preventing southern black voters from getting to the polls. That same violence followed Hayes to Washington. In 1876, the presidential inauguration was on March 4, a Sunday that year. When an inauguration date falls on a Sunday, the proceedings occur the following Monday. Hayes was sworn in twice. There are a few theories regarding the reason for the double inauguration. Because of the Sunday inauguration date and the official processing date on Monday, Congress wanted to ensure no time lapse between presidential administrations. Hayes was sworn in on March 3 in the Red Room of the White House. Also, the Grant administration did not want to provide any opportunity allowing the Tilden campaign an attempt to take the presidency if a gap existed between Grant's and Hayes' administration. Hayes' life was threatened many times between election day and the inauguration. He may have been sworn in at the White House to eliminate any outside threat. Nevertheless, Hayes was publicly inaugurated on March 5 at the Capitol.[65]

Hayes' inaugural address did not stray too far from his nomination acceptance letter when he became the Republican presidential candidate. He began his address assuring the public that despite the recently resolved controversial election, the sentiments declared in his acceptance letter remained steadfast. Hayes declared that since he was charged with governing the country, he promised to carry out his duties as defined under the Constitution. As for the South, Hayes recognized the work still to be done there, believing that a government that is a "wise, honest and peaceful local self-government," is yet to be enjoyed by all citizens but eventually will be realized when local government equally guards the interest of both races. Hayes insisted that local government submit "loyally and heartily to the Constitution and the laws—both of the nation and the states— accepting and obeying faithfully the whole Constitution as it is."Hayes attempted to sway the southern states to this mindset by stating it was his "earnest desire to regard and promote their truest interest – the interest of the white and the colored people both and equally." He planned to implement civil right reforms to eradicate the color line and distinction of the North and South and to unify a divided country.[66]

Reform was the major theme of his inaugural address. Hayes proposed civil service reform considering that civil service had become a cesspool for partisan patronage. Hayes wanted civil service to return to the intentions of the founding fathers – elected public officials should owe "their whole service to the Government and to the people" – not to their political party. Hayes acknowledged that a president is indebted to his party regarding the party's efforts to propel their candidate to elected office, but he stated that ultimately, "he serves his party best who serves the country best."[67] In notes preparing for potential reforms, Hayes proposed a Constitutional amendment that a US president should serve one term for six years without possibility of reelection. Additionally, he recommended that state governments should provide free schools with necessary federal government supplements. He also proposed that currency should be based on coins rather than paper.[68]

Article II, Section 2 of the Constitution states that the president "may require the Opinion, in writing, of the principal Officer in each of the executive Departments, upon any Subject relating to the Duties of their respective Offices."[69] This did not initiate any foundation for what is now called the President's Cabinet but, rather, allowed the president to seek advice from the secretaries of the executive offices. As most presidential traditions go, George Washington set the precedent of creating a Cabinet. Every president since has followed suit. The creation of Hayes' cabinet was no different. He collaborated with party bosses and congressional leaders to put together the most effective cabinet he could. Because of the delay in the final electoral college vote,

Hayes had not yet finalized his Cabinet by inauguration. After final discussions and deliberations, Hayes nominated William M. Evarts as Secretary of State, John Sherman as Secretary of Treasury, Carl Schurz as Secretary of the Interior, General Charles Devens as Attorney-General, D.M. Key as Postmaster General, George M. McCrary as Secretary of War, and R.W. Thompson as Secretary of the Navy. The Senate confirmed the nominations nearly unanimously. Hayes also nominated Frederick Douglass as the U.S. Marshal of the District of Columbia and after Senate confirmation, became the first African-American confirmed by the U.S Senate for a Presidential appointment.

Trust, peace, and put aside the bayonet.

CHAPTER 6

The major difficult issue President Hayes had to tackle was the remaining Reconstruction resolutions in the South, specifically in South Carolina and Louisiana. The Democrat party was already in charge of Florida. South Carolina and Louisiana were, at this time, in divided governments. The President faced potentially new elections in these two states, the legislatures taking lawful actions, leaving the self-proclaimed governors to their own devices and to remove federal troops allowing events to unfold without federal involvement. Ultimately, the president's main concern was the black citizens of those states. "The wish is to restore harmony and good feeling between sections and races. This can only be done by peaceful methods"[70] the president wrote on March 23, 1877.

"It is not the duty of the President of the United States to use the military power of the nation to decide contested elections in the States," wrote Hayes. The president believed that local self-government meant that the states must determine the outcomes of their own affairs. Current public opinion, along with Congress (the House controlled by Democrats and the Senate controlled by Republicans) was that the presence of federal troops in Southern states was not appropriate. The removal of federal troops had already begun during the Grant Administration. The president desired to restore harmony and good feelings in the South, which could only happen by "peaceful methods." The presence of troops did not represent peace.[71]

In South Carolina, Daniel Chamberlin, and Wade Hampton both had claims to the governorship of the state. Chamberlin, the Republican whose government was protected by federal troops, and Hampton, the Democrat, were summoned to Washington to meet with the president. Hampton promised to uphold black citizens' rights according to the thirteenth, fourteenth and fifteenth amendments. Hayes supported Hampton's governorship, however Chamberlain warned that ruin would come to the Republican party if the Democrats gained control. Nevertheless, Chamberlain stepped aside, handing over the statehouse to Hampton's government. Under Hayes' order, troops left on April 10, 1877. Chamberlain's warning foreshadowed the oppression, violence, and segregation suffered by Southern blacks for the next hundred years in the south.[72]

Louisiana's situation was more difficult to resolve. Republican Stephen B. Packard claimed the governorship and controlled the statehouse. Francis T. Nicholls also claimed the governorship and had control over Louisiana's state Supreme Court. The president sent a commission to Louisiana consisting of four Republicans, one Democrat, and one Independent. They were to determine if Louisiana's citizens would stand behind one united government. The president also wanted to know if Louisianans intended to maintain all citizens' rights, including black citizens, as Hayes intended from the beginning. The president had authority to intervene militarily if violence occurred, but he could not intervene in an election dispute. Secretary Evarts provided a "Second Instructions to Louisiana Commissions" stating that the president intended to remove troops in hopes of no outbreak of violence. The president left himself some margin on intervention but hoped that the state would follow through with its promise. Packard did not receive the commissions instruction well and urged Hayes to declare Packard's administration of Louisiana. However, Hayes would not intervene in that way. The president wanted the people of Louisiana to decide. A letter from hundreds of Louisianans reassured Hayes' desire for the state. The people wrote "if local self-government is given us, we pledge ourselves for the loyalty of Louisiana to the Union, for the protection of life and property and civil rights of all her citizens and for the equal benefit of her laws, without distinctions of race, color, or previous condition."[73]

The commission continued to work out a government for most of April. By April 12, the commission secured enough of a legislator that supported Nicholls. During this time, the Nicholls administration had accepted the election of 240 blacks to various positions. The administration also appointed 21 others to offices for the state. Nicholls knew that the country was watching what was happening in Louisiana and moved to placate the country. On April 20, Hayes directed the troops protecting Packard's administration to withdraw., and that withdrawal came to pass on April 24 accompanied by the reception of a cheering crowd.

The Reconstruction era for the United States was coming to a close. The president had initiated the best Southern policy for the time as the country was growing weary of Reconstruction There were, of course, detractors on both sides. There were Republicans that believed Hayes had gone back on his word to protect the black citizens of the South, and with the removal of troops, he did not fulfill his promise of protecting everyone's civil rights. The newly established

South Carolina and Louisiana governments had promised Hayes they would uphold the Thirteenth, Fourteenth and Fifteenth Amendments. Hayes believed his policies were foundationally good. "I now hope for peace, and what is equally important, security and prosperity for the colored people" Hayes wrote on April 22. "I am confident in this a good word. Time will tell."[74]

Spoils

CHAPTER 7

"We must limit and narrow the area of patronage," wrote the president after having spent the first months of his administration working on developing polices in the southern states.[75] Governmental office-seeking had been practiced since the inception of the republic. The patronage system, also referred to as the spoil system, involved campaign workers or other party-affiliated members receiving appointments in the government whenever there was a party changeover. Those that served in the winning political party would often get the choice of governmental job regardless of qualifications appointed to Cabinet offices or ambassadorships, for example. This system aimed to ensure that the winning party had people in place that support the efforts and policies of the party of the day. The spoils system became famous in 1832 when Senator William Marcy of New York stated, "to the victor belong the spoils" when defending appointments made by President Andrew Jackson.[76]

The defenders argued that this system provided an effective government, unified by a common purpose with party policy supporters at the helm of government.. However, those against the spoils system pointed out that appointments were often given to friends and supporters of the winning candidate or party, and qualifications for the appointment are overlooked. Efficiency, then, would be thrown out the window. Non-policy-bearing offices, also appointed by elected officials, carried large amounts of turnover. This system continued in the United States until after the Civil War.[77] Then candidate Rutherford B. Hayes promised during his presidential campaign to reform the US civil service sector during his administration as president. Upon becoming president, First Lady Lucy Hayes and other family members were inundated with letters from office-seekers. In fact, they received so many that Hayes and Lucy adopted a rule not to even consider the letters. "No person connected with me by blood or marriage will be appointed to office," wrote the president.[78] An anti-nepotism policy was not enacted in the United States until 1967.[79]

"We must diminish the evils of office-seeking," wrote the president. This meant stopping interference in elections by federal officers and stopping appointments dictated by congress. By this time, abuse of the system had become rampant in the United States. In his first annual message to Congress, which he wrote and sent over on December 3, 1877, The president outlined his purview on civil service reform. For civil service reform to be successful, an appointee should not be removed during their official term except for cause which their term should be for six years, or at least, different than the presidential term. Appointments should be taken out of politics and separate from that of party management work.[80]

Attempting to reform civil service in the United States would not be an easy feat. The idea was certainly popular, and the integrity of the government demanded such reform, but the idea of disrupting the ways and means of party bosses came with great resistance. Before his address to Congress, the president tried to move his reform forward. On June 22, 1877, in a letter to Sherman, Secretary of the Treasury, the president stated, "no officer should be required or permitted to take part in the management of political organizations, caucuses, conventions, or election campaigns."The officers were still allowed to vote and express their views as long as it did not interfere with their official duties. This ruling would extend to every officer of the "general Government." This action greatly satisfied civil service reforms but greatly annoyed those poised to keep things as they were. Reformers would, at times, be lukewarm to Hayes based on some appointments or removals he made. The president pointed out his own mistakes writing, "I have made mistakes in removing men who, perhaps, ought to have been retained," and mistakes happened in appointing the wrong men. The president would be more cautious in the future and resolved he would only appoint the best based on the "fullest evidence of fitness."[81] Of course, there would be times when reformers would see major progress and would be on Hayes' side. The president appointed John Marshall Harlan of Kentucky to the Supreme Court. Harlan embodied the civil service and civil rights movement for thirty-four years on the bench. [82]

It would take real legislation from Congress to make any attempt at civil service reform stick. In January 1883, Congress passed the Pendleton Civil Service Act, which Ohio Senator George H. Pendleton sponsored. Public officials would be exempt from political assessments and required competitive examinations of candidates for government positions. Although there had been many attempts at reforming civil service, including during the four years of the Hayes Administration, it was not until after the assassination of President James A. Garfield by a disgruntled office seeker in September of 1881, that Congress was willing to enact real legislation for civil services reform.[83]

Spoiling the remainder of Hayes' term as President was the focus of the newly Democratically controlled Congress. Democrats were not alone in this pursuit. A handful of Republicans, who were against Hayes' attempts at reforming the spoils system, were on the hunt to undermine the administration. With bad blood boiling between the president and Senator Roscoe Conkling, who chaired the Senate Committee on Commerce (the committee that nominations were referred to), blocked the president's nominees for the New York customhouse.[84] The president lamented "in the language of the press, 'Senator Conkling has won a great victory of the Administration." However, the president did not feel defeated. "But the end is not yet. I am right and shall not give up the contest."[85]

During the Civil War, paper money, not gold-backed, was issued to help finance the Union. At the close of the war, there was a push from the Republicans to retire the paper money or greenbacks as they were referred to. The Supreme Court, at the time, ruled that greenbacks were constitutional and could resume as legal tender. As a reaction to that ruling, hard money (gold and silver) advocates pushed to retire the paper money resulting in the Resumption Act of 1875. The Resumption Act called for the Secretary of the Treasury to begin to call the paper money back on January 1, 1879. Before the January deadline, there was $430 million in greenbacks in circulation in the United States. The Act demanded that greenbacks be reduced to $300 million in circulation by January 1, 1879.[86]

The president has always favored a return to the gold standard opposing the continued circulation of the greenbacks. Believing that a sound monetary policy was basing currency on a stable gold standard. The president did not necessarily oppose the coining of silver, maintaining that the gold ratio was appropriate so as not to cause inflation. In November of 1877, The House passed a silver bill that called for unlimited silver dollar coinage. The Senate added an amendment, which provided discretion of the treasury secretary to coin two to four million silver dollars a month.[87] In February of 1878, the Senate passed what became known as the Bland-Allison Act, which Hayes was determined to veto. The president stated, "the faith of the nation was to be violated—the obligation of contracts was impaired by the law." However, the veto was overridden by Congress. This veto made the Bland-Allison Act law.[88]

The Democrats, in control of Congress, moved to discredit the president by developing the Potter Investigation. Named after Representative to New York, Clarkson N. Potter, the investigation intended was to find fraud in the Louisiana and Florida elections in 1876. The president offered his opinion on establishing the investigation as "a partisan proceeding for merely partisan ends. If the Republicans manage well their side of the controversy, I suspect it will damage its authors,"[89] which it did. On June 14, 1878, Congress passed two resolutions "denying that Congress, the courts, or any tribunal could reverse the delectation of the Forty-fourth Congress that Hayes and Wheeler had been elected."[90]

EPILOGUE

The thermometer read 30 degrees at Spiegel Grove on March 10, 1881. The former president walked rapidly around his home during the sunrise. During a walk to the depot where he was weighed, coming in at 192 pounds, resolved to lose five pounds. [91]

Hayes was determined to follow through on his commitment to seek one term as President. It could be argued that with the climate of Congress and the reforms Hayes sought during his administration, he would have only received one term. However, Hayes was determined to only govern during his term and not be distracted with also having to campaign. His governing would then be tainted with hesitation having to consider how his actions would affect his upcoming election.

Hayes was instrumental in picking his successor. James A. Garfield was nominated for the Republican nomination for President in Chicago on June 11, 1880. Hayes said the "nomination at Chicago was the best that was possible. It is altogether good." Garfield was a self-made man. Hayes believed that his life and struggles, presented thoroughly, in facts, and representation would carry him well to the presidency. Hayes suggested that every twenty years, character is what a successful campaign can be built on; remembering those of Jackson in 1820, Harrison in 1840, Lincoln in 1860 and now in 1880, Garfield. Garfield would be elected "without hitch or difficulty."[92]

In a letter to William Henry Smith, the man who wrote telling Hayes to run for Governor of Ohio, the former president wrote:

> "I step out of the dust and confusion of getting into orderly living after our six years' absence, to ask, 'Are you happy, and do you know anything?'
>
> With us time passes swiftly and pleasantly. The escape from bondage into freedom is grateful indeed to my feelings. The equanimity of temper which has enabled me to bear without discompose the vexations and anxieties that every day brought with it during my term in office, no doubt relieved me from a great part of the strain upon the faculties which has broken down so many of my predecessors. But the burden, even with my constitutional cheerfulness, has not been light one. I am glad to be a freedman.
>
> "Now a word to you. My obligations to you I do not attempt to measure or to describe. You were at the cradle, and you have followed the hearse 'of this ambitious life.' I know that to you it has not brought the reward or the satisfaction which you deserve to have. No man ever had a more sincere, a more judicious, and more unselfish friend than, in this matter, I have in you. You have been generous, considerate, and forgiving. With all my heart I thank you and be you to believe me your friend ever."93

Sincerely,
R.B. Hayes

ACKNOWLEDGMENTS

In case you were wondering, I made a choice to leave that promotion and by a stroke of Divine intervention, was able to assume my previous role and for the first time in my career feel satisfied and fulfilled in what I do and who I work for.

Now, here is where I can provide another example of humility. I did not, could not, have done this project on my own. Thank you to my wonderful, supportive, and intelligent wife Abby. Without your support and sacrifice, this would not be possible.

Keeping it in the family, to my parents, Bill and Barbara, thank you for your never-ending love and support in my education and in my passions. Thank you to the best editor, my Mother-in-Law, Nancy. Thank you for sacrificing your time to work on my project.

To my boss and great friend, Beth—you took a chance on me, not once, but twice! I will be forever grateful. You display integrity, humility, and accountability every day. #DreamTeam

To a former boss and current great friend, Jared – You showed me what it is like to have integrity as a leader every day. Thank you for investment in me and your continued mentorship and friendship.

Thank you to the historians who have invested in researching and documenting the lives and decisions of our presidents. A special thank you to Ari Hoogenboom for doing extensive research to write *Rutherford B. Hayes: Warrior and President* and *The Presidency of Rutherford B. Hayes*. These resources were invaluable. Thank you to the employees of the Rutherford B Hayes Presidential Library and Museum. Your willingness to help me navigate the many resources of Hayes was incredibly helpful.

To Igniting Souls Publishing Company, without your willingness to take a chance on me, my dream would have never become a reality. Thank you!

Thank you to my accountability team – my friends and family. Without all of you asking when this would be finished, it would not have been! I am very grateful.

ENDNOTES

1 Eragula, Rahul. "Humility in Leadership." Advances in Economics and Business Management, 2015. https://rahuleragula.com/wp-content/uploads/2020/09/humilty-in-leadership-by-rahul-eragula.pdf.

2 Editors, History.Com. "Whig Party - Definition, Beliefs & Leaders." History.com, 2022. https://www.history.com/topics/19th-century/whig-party.

3 Editors, History.com. "Republican Party Founded." History.com, 2021. https://www.history.com/this-day-in-history/republican-party-founded.

4 Hayes, Rutherford B. "Diaries and Letters of Rutherford B Hayes." Volume I Chapter XII, https://resources.ohiohistory.org/hayes/browse/chapteriv.html

5 Hayes, *Diaries,* VI, ChIV

6 Hayes, *Diaries,* VI, ChIV

7 Hayes, *Diaries,* VI, ChVII

8 Johnston, Robert D. "Rutherford B. Hayes: Life before the Presidency." Miller Center, September 28, 2020. https://miller-center.org/president/hayes/life-before-the-presidency.

9 Hoogenboom, Ari. "'Rutherford B. Hayes and African-Americans' by Ari Hoogenboom." Rutherford B. Hayes Presidential Library & Museums, n.d. https://www.rbhayes.org/hayes/rutherford-b.-hayes-and-african-americans-by-ari-hoogenboom/.

10 Hoogenboom, *Rutherford B. Hayes and African-Americans*

11 Hoogenboom, *Rutherford B. Hayes and African-Americans*

12 Hayes, *Diaries,* VI, ChXII

13 Hayes, *Diaries,* VI, ChXII

14 Hayes, *Diaries,* VIII, ChXXVI

15 Chesnut, Robert, and Joan O'C Hamilton. "Chapter 2." Essay. In Intentional Integrity: How Smart Companies Can Lead An Ethical Revolution, 34–34. New York, NY: St. Martin's Press, an imprint of St. Martin's Publishing Group, 2020.

16 Hayes, *Diaries,* VI, ChXII

17 Hayes, *Diaries,* VII, ChXIV

18 Hayes, *Diaries,* IV, ChXIV

19 Howard, J. Q. Life, public services and select speeches of Rutherford B. Hayes. Cincinnati, OH: R. Clarke, 1876

20 Hayes, *Diaries,* VII, ChXLIV

21 Hayes, *Diaries,* II, ChXXIV

22 Hayes, *Diaries,* III, ChXXVI

23 Hayes, *Diaries,* III, ChXXVI

24 Hayes, *Diaries,* III, ChXXVI

25 Hayes, *Diaries,* III, ChXXVI

26 Hayes, *Diaries,* III, ChXXVI

27 Hayes, *Diaries,* III, ChXXVI

28 Raymond, Jonathan. "Do You Understand What Accountability Really Means?" Harvard Business Review, October 13, 2016. https://hbr.org/2016/10/do-you-understand-what-accountability-really-means?registration=success.

29 Hayes, *Diaries,* III, ChXXVI

30 Hayes, *Diaries,* III, ChXXVI

31 Hayes, *Diaries,* III, ChXXVI

32 Hayes, *Diaries,* III, ChXXVI

33 Howard, J. Q. *Life, public services and select speeches of Rutherford B. Hayes.* Cincinnati, OH: R. Clarke, 1876, 168.

34 Howard, *Life, public services and select speeches of Rutherford B. Hayes,* 168

35 Howard, *Life, public services and select speeches of Rutherford B. Hayes,* 168

36 Hayes, *Diaries,* III, ChXXVI

37 Hayes, *Diaries,* III, ChXXVI

38 Hayes, *Diaries,* III, ChXXVI

39 "15th Amendment to the U.S. Constitution: Voting Rights (1870)." National Archives and Records Administration, n.d. https://www.archives.gov/milestone-document s/15th-amendment#:~:text=Passed%20by%20Congress%20 February%2026,men%20the%20right%20to%20vote.

40 Hoogenboom, Ari. "Governor Essay. In Rutherford B. Hayes: Warrior and President, 218-220. Lawrence, Kansas: University Press of Kansas, 1995.

41 Hayes, *Diaries,* III, ChXXVIII

42 Norwood, Candice. "Do Iowa Caucus Winners Become President? History Shows Mixed Results." PBS. Public Broadcasting Service, February 6, 2020. https://www.pbs.org/ newshour/politics/do-iowa-caucus-winners-become-presiden t-history-shows-mixed-results.

43 Jason Bernert, Lenny Bronner. "Super Tuesday 2020: Live Results and Exit Polling." The Washington Post. WP Company, June 1, 2020. https://www.washingtonpost.com/elections/ election-results/super-tuesday/.

44 "Ulysses Grant's Bid for a Third Term." LiveJournal, 2017. https://potus-geeks.livejournal.com/840321.html.

45 Hayes, *Diaries,* III, ChXXXII

46 Hoogenboom, *Rutherford B. Hayes: Warrior and President*, 238.

47 Hayes, *Diaries,* III, ChXXXII

48 Hayes, *Diaries,* III, ChXXXI

49 Hayes, *Diaries,* III, ChXXXI

50 Hayes, *Diaries,* III, ChXXXII

51 Hayes, *Diaries,* III, ChXXXII

52 Chapter 3 was a summary of a first-hand account of the Republican Convention in 1876 by William C. Cochran. Cochran, William C. "Hayes Historical Journal: Dear Mother." Rutherford B. Hayes Presidential Library & Museums. Accessed August 2, 2021. https://www.rbhayes.org/research/hayes-historical-journal-dear-mother/.

53 Cochran, William C. "Hayes Historical Journal: Dear Mother." Rutherford B. Hayes Presidential Library & Museums. Accessed August 2, 2021. https://www.rbhayes.org/research/hayes-historical-journal-dear-mother/.

54 Hayes, *Diaries,* III, ChXXXII

55 Howard, *Life, public services and select speeches of Rutherford B. Hayes*, 158-159.

56 Hoogenboom, *Rutherford B. Hayes: Warrior and President*, 265.

57 Hayes, *Diaries,* III, ChXXXIII

58 Hayes, *Diaries,* III, ChXXXIII

59 Hoogenboom, *Rutherford B. Hayes: Warrior and President*, 270-271.

60 Hayes, *Diaries,* III, ChXXXIII

61 Hayes, *Diaries,* III, ChXXXVI

62 Hayes, *Diaries,* III, ChXXXIII

63 "Frequently Asked Questions on the 1876 Election." Rutherford B. Hayes Presidential Library & Museums, n.d. https://www.rbhayes.org/hayes/frequently-asked-questions-on-the-1876-election/.

64 "Frequently Asked Questions on the 1876 Election."

65 Editors, History.com. "Rutherford B. Hayes Is Inaugurated in a Private Ceremony." History.com, 2021. https://www.history. com/this-day-in-history/rutherford-b-hayes-is-inaugurated-i n-a-private-ceremony.

66 Hoogenboom, *The Presidency of Rutherford B. Hayes*, 53.

67 Hoogenboom, *The Presidency of Rutherford B. Hayes*, 54.

68 Hayes, *Diaries*, III, ChXXXV

69 Article II Section 2 - Constitution Annotated | Congress.gov, n.d. https://constitution.congress.gov/browse/article-2/section-2/.

70 Hayes, *Diaries*, III, ChXXXV

71 Hayes, *Diaries*, III, ChXXXV

72 Trefousse, Hans Louis. Essay. In *Rutherford B. Hayes*, 89–93. New York, NY: Times Books, 2002.

73 Hoogenboom, *Rutherford B. Hayes: Warrior and President*, 311–11.

74 Hayes, *Diaries*, III, ChXXXV

75 Hayes, *Diaries*, III, ChXXXV

76 Tikkanen, Amy. "Spoils System." Encyclopedia Britannica. https://www.britannica.com/topic/spoils-system.

77 Tikkanen, "Spoils System."

78 Hayes, *Diaries*, III, ChXXXV

79 "5 U.S. Code § 3110 - Employment of Relatives; Restrictions." Legal Information Institute.. https://www.law.cornell.edu/ uscode/text/5/3110.

80 Hayes, *Diaries*, III, ChXXXV

81 Hayes, *Diaries*, III, ChXXXV

82 Hoogenboom, *The Presidency of Rutherford B. Hayes*, 137–137.

83 Smith, Thomas A. "Hayes Historical Journal: 1883 - 1983 Civil Service Act." Rutherford B. Hayes Presidential Library & Museums, 1984. https://www.rbhayes.org/research/ hayes-historical-journal-1883-1983-civil-service-act/.

84 Hoogenboom, *Rutherford B. Hayes: Warrior and President*, 352–53.

85 Hayes, *Diaries,* III, ChXXXV

86 Young, Grace. "Resumption Act of 1875." Encyclopedia Britannica, 2016. https://www.britannica.com/topic/Resumption-Act-of-1875.

87 Hoogenboom. *Rutherford B. Hayes: Warrior and President,* 356-356.

88 Hoogenboom. *Rutherford B. Hayes: Warrior and President,* 358-359.

89 Hayes, *Diaries,* III, ChXXXVI

90 Hoogenboom. *Rutherford B. Hayes: Warrior and President,* 368-368.

91 Hayes, *Diaries,* IV ChXXXIX

92 Hayes, *Diaries,* III ChXXXVIII

93 Hayes, *Diaries,* IV ChXXXIX

Made in the USA
Columbia, SC
23 October 2023

8faa5034-0036-4beb-99f3-9f5aaff07d12R01